Destiny's Trouble

A true story

Connie S. Blosser

PublishAmerica
Baltimore

First printing

Softcover 9781462693412
PUBLISHED BY PUBLISHAMERICA, LLLP
www.publishamerica.com
Baltimore

Printed in the United States of America

It was midway thru the fifth grade, one day, Destiny was told by her parents they would be moving and to a new school, she would soon be going to.

Much to her surprise, the schools had nothing alike; things would be severely changing, and it would be in her life rearranging.

The first day of school Destiny woke up, with great expectations, and ended up unlike she anticipated. She looked thru the big picture window and seen the new paper boy, but when the paperboy seen her brother, he became annoyed. It was much of a surprise to him to find he was handicapped. And Destiny's first day of school the kids laughed, because her brother was handicapped.

Many days would pass, and they would still laugh, weeks passed, how could this behavior last? Months and years pass by; Destiny kept asking God....why? God didn't answer her back, and it got worse than just laughs. They became attacks, one day pushed down in the snow lying on her back, she said, "I have to fight back!" Not knowing how to fight back, she attacked back, punched someone's teeth, nose bleeds, and received spankings.

Just before dark, a fight broke out in a local park, teasing, taunting, cruelness and vocal abuse. Fists throwing, and then both went home, yet no one at home would be told. The following morning, just before class starting, Destiny was called to the front of the class to apologize....and her answer was, "Why?" The teacher replied, "You were in a fight and you need to apologize!" She refused because of the constant abuse, the teacher replied, "Come to the front of the class, apologize or reach for your ankles!"

As she reached for her ankles he grabbed his board from the table. Nothing happened to the aggressor of the fight; she held back the tears from her eyes. As she sat in her seat, she thought how can this be? How can all of this happen to me? It doesn't have anything to do with me. Can't they see my brother means everything to me?

Years pass, **but her anger lasts**. High school comes and goes and then the first class reunion is known. A fellow class mate asks Destiny, "Are you going to our class reunion?" She replied, "No, I never really enjoyed school why would I want to see anyone and go back?" Her friend knew her long time struggle and attacks, he replied, "do you know that very boy that was your paperboy that made life so hard because of your brother is now pushing his dad in a wheel chair, like your brothers?"

Destiny bowed her head in remorse. Knowing when she gave up the battle, it became the Lords. And as she looked at her belly, with a baby inside, a change of heart was more needed at this time. The best time to change, is before the start of a new day and begin to understand, beyond our control even things can change.

We never know what can happen when we treat others without compassion. What might not be our compassion and understanding might be our destiny. The bible says, "Do to others as you would have them do to you."

1 Samuel 17:47

And everyone assembled here will know that the LORD rescues his people, but not with sword and spear. This is the **LORD's battle**, and he will give you to us!"

Matthew 25:44

"They also will answer, 'Lord, when did we see you hungry or thirsty or a stranger or needing clothes or sick or in prison, and did not <u>help</u> you?'

Matthew 25:45

"He will reply, 'I tell you the truth, whatever you did not do for one of the least of these, you did not do for me.'

Luke 6:31

Do to others as you would have them do to you.

CPSIA information can be obtained
at www.ICGtesting.com
Printed in the USA
LVIC052151220413
330392LV00001B